Returning Natural:

The History, Healing, and Holistic Health of

Black Hair

Returning Natural:

The History, Healing, and Holistic Health of Black Hair

- Nikki Taylor -

The Return Natural Company, LLC

Atlanta, GA

Printed in the United States of America

First Printing, 2014

Second Edition, 2016

ISBN-13: 978-0692339954

Published by The Return Natural Company, LLC

Cover Design: Darius Armour

DEDICATION

This book is dedicated to my two beautiful daughters, Nikkayla and Nyema. Thank you for being my reason. Always shine bright.

TABLE OF CONTENTS

The Holistic Health of Black Hair

SANKOFA

Sankofa is an Akan word from West Africa that translates to "reach back and get it". This concept encourages us to return to our past for guidance on ways to pursue a successful future. When reaching back, we come to know who we are, what we are capable of, why the connection to our past is important and how we can implement changes for advancement. We connect with a divine intelligence that not only gives us the guidance we need to navigate throughout this dimension, but we come to understand, respect and love ourselves unapologetically. To embrace the spirit of Sankofa is to reclaim a legacy that was stolen. It is the very essence that connects us back to our roots and keeps us connected to the source of creation. It reminds us that we are innately powerful and possess the ability to conquer and manifest. Through reaching back, we live.

> This is more than a fad. It's more than fashion. It's more than just another silly woman thing.

> **This. Is. A. Movement.**

Black Power

Afro, Electrical.

Locs, Supreme.

Antennas conversing with the sun.

Transmitting instructions for the chosen one.

Kinks, Metaphysical.

Curls, Majestic.

A thousand petals emanating light.

Revealing direction for travel through the night.

Braids, Kemetic.

Twists, Aboriginal.

Trends outlining the presence of royalty.

Embracing the roots, showing pride and loyalty.

Confused by the robust radiation.

Fear masked as coercion for assimilation.

Relax.

Relate.

Release the power that is black.

Submission is destruction; it's time to get it back!

Afros ignite a mighty revolution.

Locs guide the path of purpose.

Kinks support cerebral liberation.

Curls speak the language of destiny.

Braids mimic ancestral crowns.

Twists say that we were great before we knew anything else existed.

Don't ever get it twisted.

PREFACE

Congratulations!!! *Throws confetti and blows a paper whistle.*

Yes, all of that celebration is just for you! Why? Because you've picked up this book and have officially expressed interest in joining The Return. Whether you've already transitioned to embrace your natural hair, are considering a transition or just looking for a deeper understanding of your completed transition, your desire to return natural is to be commended.

This acceptance of your natural beauty is more than a simple change of hairstyle. It's the beginning of a journey toward self-discovery, impeccable health, and a flourishing lifestyle. It's a symbol that informs those around you of your confidence. It's an act that connects you to your divine self and inspires spiritual elevation.

Within the last decade, there has been an influx of black women "going natural." This phrase is commonly used to refer to the act of allowing one's hair to grow in its natural state as opposed to permanently straightening it with a chemical process. Numerous social media sites, viral Internet videos, blogs, and hair forums are packed full of information on this process. Many women have devoted extensive amounts of time and energy into learning the best techniques used to care for black hair, perfecting natural hair-styles, and even creating their own hair products.

You can learn just about any and everything you'll ever need to know about going natural by simply typing the phrase into your favorite search engine.

❖ You'll learn the number/letter combination that describes how tight or loose your curl pattern is.

❖ You'll be inundated with opinions on the best and worst products to use on your hair type.

❖ You'll learn how to braid it up, twist it up, coil it up, curl it up, and roll it up.

❖ You'll connect with others as they journey through their natural hair process.

❖ You'll find contests that give prizes to as-sist you on your journey.

❖ You'll learn all of the technical "do's and don'ts"
of natural hair.

❖ You'll find conferences and social events to attend in praise of natural hair.

❖ You'll join an enormous community filled with support and approval for your decision.

You should never have a question left unanswered as you embrace your transition. And because there's a plethora of knowledge on what to do when you go natural, you won't find any of that information within these pages.

❖ I won't walk you through how to style your cute little Afro that's made a bold appearance after   cutting off the over-processed ends of your hair.
❖ I won't run down a list of my favorite natural hair bloggers and point you to videos that teach you all of the "correct" natural hair terminology.
❖ I won't even tell you about all of the stages you and your hair will go through when you decide to embark on your journey.

Nope! I won't do that simply because there are enough beautifully talented individuals who've already done that for you. They've written you a perfect blueprint on what to do once you finally see the natural hair type and texture that's been secretly hidden away for so many years. But most importantly, I won't do it because this book is not about *going* natural. This book is about *returning natural*.

What's the difference? Let's start with a simple definition:

Going: *The act of leaving a place. Used to describe a situation in which you are trying to make progress or do something.*

Returning: *To go back again. To go back in thought, practice, or condition.*

If we take these definitions into consideration, the difference between the process of "going natural" and the process of "returning natural" emerges.

Understanding this difference places a greater value on the process of the return. And after analyzing the integrity of each journey, you may also come to understand why going natural has been considered the latest trend as opposed to a powerful movement within the black community.

Going natural encourages women to stop chemically straightening their hair and try to advance along their natural hair journey.

In this process, learning a fail-proof technique for creating the perfect frizz-free ringlets or well-defined hairstyle equals success. It encourages them to put forth a great effort in mimicking the hair texture of their favorite curly haired crush. Some may even find themselves straining to accomplish this, creating a stressful environment for their hair as it is labeled "unmanageable" or "ugly." If taken lightly, going natural can eventually render your hair another cutesy accessory to a culturally chic outfit.

Returning natural prompts you to go back from whence you came. It requires you to remove yourself from the constraints of societal imagery and embrace the roots of your genealogy. It encourages you to revere your hair the way it grew from your head when you made your entrance into the world.

The focus should not be on the struggle to leave your relaxed hair and try to get to your natural state, but more so on the act of proudly *returning* to your origin.

This message is about embracing the process with that focus at the forefront of your transition. We must begin to return natural and not only go back to our natural hair texture, but also go back to the natural thoughts, practices, and principles of our ancestors.

"But why is this necessary?" you might ask. In a country where European images are upheld as the standard for beauty, it becomes vitally important for us to begin redefining that ideology within our own community.

Our children are bombarded with television shows, toys, and neat paraphernalia that depict "cool kids" who don't resemble their own image. Our most popular magazines and favorite media advertisements portray models with a very distinct sex appeal that leaves us questioning our very own nature of sacred sexual energy.

If you're reluctant to accept this statement as truth, simply type the word "beauty" into your favorite search engine and observe for yourself the images that populate. Now try "pretty," "gorgeous," and "sexy."

What do you notice? Do you see that the presence of natural black beauty is virtually non-existent in those search results? With or without processed hair, it seems to appear that we just don't fit within societal beauty standards.

And that reason alone is exactly why this message is necessary. Because we don't fit society's ideal image of European beauty standards, it is necessary for us to understand the issues at hand, address them accordingly, change our mindsets as individuals, and begin to redefine that standard.

The bronzed skin, prominent physical features, and natural hair texture of black women is the most beautiful image that anyone could ever behold. Sadly, because society tells us otherwise, many of us have failed to grasp that concept.

From school handbooks to corporate dress code policies, it is clear that society is constantly telling us that the hair that grows naturally from our heads is "radical," "distracting," or "inappropriate."

The media consistently reminds us that our natural image isn't widely accepted and many of us have embraced this as truth.

The purpose of this work is to empower you to walk boldly into the world with your head held high as a Queen of African descent. Through individual awareness and self-acceptance, you can play a substantial role in redefining the standard of beauty that black women are judged by.

This type of elevation requires more than a simple change in the way we wear our hair. It requires a drastic change in the way we think and operate as well. This is required to truly understand the movement that is taking place during this present time. Many of us are overlooking it, because we are too busy buying every hair product that has the word "natural" immaculately placed across the front of it. But if we stop for a moment and realize what is happening, we will definitely recognize a spiritual shift taking place.

The transition of thousands of women across the globe now embracing their natural hair that was once labeled "uncivilized" is, to say the very least, a true movement.

My mission is to highlight that movement and encourage an unyielding sense of pride to accompany your transition. I want to abolish the initial fear that so many women encounter when considering their return. I want to be an asset in the process of redefining the standards of beauty for all women of color.

But in order to understand this notion, one must be free and understand the essence of freedom in its entirety. Freedom of thought. Freedom of spirit. Freedom of repression. An open heart and free mind receives, from spirit, a word that one may not have known through flesh or tradition.

Therefore, to gain a solid interpretation of this message, one must be willing to grow from that which we've come to know as comfortable and enter into a new realm of knowledge.

We must be open to growing beyond that

which we've previously known as the history of black people and open up to a truth that predates the trans-Atlantic slave trade. We must grow beyond modern-day media portrayals, celebrities, and the image of the masses and embrace the authentic beauty that we find there.

We must accept this movement as a spiritual liberation and stand as leaders for the change necessary amongst our people.

Allowing the light from your return to illuminate the world is vital. Without it, we will continue to perish within our community.

Elevation begins with education. You must give more than a mere, "I'm a black woman and I'm proud of my hair texture." You must educate yourself and know yourself. You must connect with your true history, begin a healing that transcends generations, and embrace the sovereign spirit of your ancestors. You must begin to operate as the Queen that you are and take your position to rule.

In this book, we will return to our roots and discuss the nature and importance of a history that precedes what we routinely acknowledge. We will return to our wounds and address the present mindset of bondage that we as a people find ourselves in today. We will return to the ways of our ancestors and embrace the wonderful qualities of nature and all it gives to help us care for the health of our hair holistically. And lastly, we will return to our divine essence of origin and fully embrace the journey, thus allowing us to uncover the supernatural power that lies within our royal crown.

PASSION IS PURPOSE

My background is rooted in black hair. It's always been an extremely important part of my life. I stumbled across this love as a desperate eighth grader who really wanted to get her hair braided, but didn't have the money to do so. I set out to accomplish the hairstyle myself and instantly realized that I had a natural talent. I put my fresh braids in two ponytails and added red ribbons; everybody at school loved it! "Who did your hair?" they kept asking me; and thus began the side-hustle of a very ambitious young lady.

Eventually, the word got out about "the little middle school girl" running a business out of her moms garage and I was introduced to a master cosmetologist to help foster my interest. "Would you like to come hang out with me today?" she asked. "Yeah!" I said ecstatically. She took me to her place of business and I observed her catering to clients with love and care. I could tell that she took her work very seriously. As I watched her moved intensely, I couldn't help but notice that her assistant did not work with the same enthusiasm. By the end of the day I was convinced that she needed me as her sidekick and I eventually got up the nerve to tell her so. She smiled at my innocent attempt at manifesting my desires and we ended the day with dinner and a divine connection.

The next weekend, I returned back to the hair salon at 5:00 a.m. on Saturday morning as instructed, and began working as a shampoo assistant.

I spent most of my adolescent years tightly attached to hair stylists and barbers. Growing up in a salon environment was everything to me. While most teens were running off to parties and having fun at the neighborhood hang out, I was busy nurturing my talents and falling in love with destiny. And even after graduating from high school, receiving a college degree and starting a corporate career, I still found myself assisting on the weekends and freelancing whenever I had any available time.

That background taught me to love the versatility that is black hair. I adore how we can go from kinky to curly to straight and back again. We can put beads in our hair, add swirls of pink and purple, adorn it with signs, and even add lights! (Okay, those last few are probably only acceptable at artistic hair shows, but you get the point.) We can do things to our hair that others look at in amazement. You know this as truth because they're always asking if they can touch it or seeking an explanation as to "how" we created a particular style. Our hair is fabulous in every aspect.

After many years of searching for my purpose, exploring my place in this world and finding a good fit for my skills and talents. I came to know black hair in its natural state as my divine calling. Now operating as a professional loctician and holistic hair care consultant, I am able to allow my love for kinks and curls to pave a way for me to educate and help redefine the standards of beauty for women of color.

Returning natural is not a campaign against a particular hairstyle. It's not about stating that anyone who hasn't decided to embrace their natural appearance is basking in self-hatred. It's not a work that casts judgment or condemns. It's the opportunity for us to institute change and just in case you needed it, it's your approval to boldly embrace your natural beauty.

> **We must begin to educate well beyond what we've always known. Seek out the truth. Find ourselves there.**

HiStory

A young soul, stolen from the arms of his mother, forced to enter a point of no return.

Linked forcefully to his brother and told promises that will be broken.

Broken. Bones, confidence and pride.

He follows the sign that reads "hell this way."

He walks with his head to the ground as RA kisses the top of his head.

Head. Shoulders. Knees. Toes. All rotting away.

Filling the darkness with a stench of death.

He tries to break free. The mission is proven impossible.

The waves of the ocean carry his destiny.

Arriving to a land his ancestors have already deemed familiar.

SOLD! A life stamped with four bold letters.

Letters. Creating words that attempt to erase a nation.

Desperately seeking abandonment.

Delivering imagery that subdues the masses and proclaims its own.

Own. Belonging to an individual. Property. Possession.

Self-appointed power. Lies. Fear of rebellion is truth.

Man minus culture equals captivity.

Equals superiority.

He cries out in pain and I hear the triumphant beat of his drum.

His flesh is divided and I see the nectar of royalty.

My spirit weeps as I explore his sacrifice, yet I am reminded.

Reminded that he once wore a crown of gold and gemstones divine.

Reminded that he often ate from the goodness of the land and walked through paradise singing praises to the Almighty.

Reminded that his spirit was once at peace and that love was all the religion he'd ever need.

Reminded of his divine intelligence and I am fascinated.

They called him a slave.

They drew him defeated.

I call him a King.

I paint him supreme.

THE BRIEF HISTORY OF

BLACK HAIR

ANCESTRAL BEINGS

We cannot begin to speak about the history of black hair, or black people, without first thanking our great ancestors for their ultimate sacrifices. The reality of the turmoil faced during the enslavement of our people is one that I believe can never truly be known, yet somehow, so many of them endured and pressed on. For their strength, their unbreakable spirits and their supreme existence, we must always give thanks, honor, praise, and respect.

The trans-Atlantic slave trade is a topic that will always create a wave of emotions. Our feelings can quickly intensify from zero to twenty when we bring up the pain that dwells within that era. There are so many different opinions that may arise when we talk about the enslavement of African people.

There are those who believe it is merely a small point in the time of our history and that we should be looking more to our future than our past:

"That was so long ago! We need to move on."

"That's what's wrong with black people. We're

always bringing up slavery! Let it go!"

"We just need to forget those horrible memories; it's all over now!"

The people who utter these remarks want to ignore the pain and dispel the arguments that stem from this topic of discussion. They want to ignore what is, in truth, the root cause of many of today's issues.

To them, slavery has absolutely nothing to do with them personally and they'd rather not be bothered with the stigma that has been placed on their group of people. They wish to disassociate themselves with this history as much as possible.

It is safe to say that this type of thinking breeds a self-loathing mentality and ultimately creates bondage within the black community. It has us:

- ❖ Picking "teams" to play for based on how light or dark the pigment of our skin is.
- ❖ Obsessing over hair that was cut from another individual's head and tacking it on to our own in hopes of feeling beautiful.

❖ Making sure the length of the hair is below our waistline and of a texture that bears no resemblance to our natural hair.

❖ Damaging our own health, scalp and hair follicles with years of chemical treatments to make our hair "more manageable."

❖ Hating our hair and calling it ugly while simultaneously labeling "nappy" a derogatory term.

To reject an interest in your ancestors' past is to reject the opportunity to obtain knowledge of Self. Without it, you cannot and will not flourish. You must know where you've come from to know where you are going.

On the other side are those who consider slavery the beginning of their history. In their mind, their culture only goes as far back as the book that they read in grade school.

"Look how far we've come!" they often say. To them, the black community has "arrived." We can eat at the table with our white co-workers. We can obtain degrees and apply for jobs without blatant discrimination. And we can openly embrace interracial relationships. To them, we are equal.

The problem with this thought process begins

with the notion that slavery is the beginning of your history. If your beginning is filled with memories of torment, anything thereafter that doesn't mimic that situation will appear to be progressive. This, however, is simply not the truth about our community.

With the help of some phenomenally anointed leaders we have made great strides since emancipation, but we are not completely progressive.

Progress is not an entire people being stripped of their identity. It is not being brainwashed to believe that your natural image is not acceptable as a standard for beauty in the country of which you reside. Nor is it a people divided, confused, and uneducated about their true history.

And yes, the above is relevant even today. The media, government, judicial system, corporate structure, financial class system, and education system make it clear that although we, as black people, are free to live in a country, the parameters by which we are able to do so are a bit skewed.

To reject the memory of ancestors or to reference slavery as the beginning of a cultural history can directly affect the self-esteem and value of a people.

Subconsciously, and even consciously in some cases, many reject their natural image and freely embrace that of societal norms. They reject dark skin complexions because it reminds them of the ancestors working hard in the fields as the sun beat down on their bodies. They reject "nappy" hair because it reminds them of the maidservants tasked to cater to the master and his family. For some, their features equate pain.

However, if we begin to take the true history of our great ancestors into account, the image of self will instantly appear more glorious. We must remember that our ancestors were great and royal people! They were a people filled with rich culture. They were the beginning of life as the world knew it and they gave birth to a foundation that other cultures would use to establish structure within their own communities. Understanding this truth opens a portal for tremendous elevation.

EMBRACING REJECTION

Sadly, it appears that we are the only people who are unaware of our true history. We don't know who we are, but many others know the truth of our ancestral greatness. In my observation, I've come to understand that as a strategic process. People with minimal knowledge of self are people without direction, quick to follow whoever appears to be paving the way toward success. And because of this, we've somehow learned to live while embracing a culture that resembles nothing close to that of our own. We've learned to craft ourselves after an art form we were never meant to resemble.

We try to mimic the images, lifestyle practices, religions, activities, and standards of a people that we will never fully connect with. If you do not know who you are and where you've come from, you are easily susceptible to thought manipulation. And because of this, you'll eventually believe that you are not enough naturally. You'll honestly think that you have to change certain things about yourself to "fit in," "advance," "be accepted," or even "be successful." Your brain will have been washed with lies and deceit to keep you stagnant as you fraudulently appear to make progress.

We can pinpoint a time in history when this ideology became rampant in the United States. In the early 1900's, a product emerged that encouraged people of color to "fix their appearance." This product was a called a "relaxer," a chemical designed to permanently alter the natural texture of black hair. The creation of this process motivated blacks to straighten their hair so that they'd look "better" as they walked around this country with freedom. It encouraged blacks to work harder at fitting in so they could achieve prosperity and success. That addictive substance with a creamy consistency was extremely instrumental in advancing the rejection of our own heritage and culture.

Fast-forward a few decades and we've now added a massive obsession with weaves—sewn, glued and clipped onto our heads. We've fallen in love with extensions that must touch the top of our buttocks and possess a wave pattern like that of the ocean. The more expensive the bundle of hair, the more successful we feel. The more our curl flips with perfection around our face, the more we connect with a coveted status of celebrity

We've even advanced this process to move

beyond synthetic fibers. Many of us are now lusting after the long locks of women who inhabit another culture. We happily purchase the hair that was cut off during religious and cultural rituals and weave it onto our own heads. And because energy never dies, we willingly connect with the trials, hurts, pains, sorrows, and tribulations of another's life and operate in it on a daily basis. We're voluntarily taking on circumstances that weren't originally drafted into our blueprint.

This type of control is so subtly powerful because it makes us feel that without long, expensive, straight or wavy "virgin" hair, we aren't good enough for high-ranking corporate jobs, solid romantic relationships, or meeting other personal goals. So many of us tie every facet of our destiny up into the simple strands of hair on our heads, when in fact, we are more than that.

Now let me be clear: I am in no way bashing any person who creates, purchases, applies, or wears a relaxer. I'm not judging the woman who currently refuses to be seen in public without her weave. Everyone has their own personal journey and everyone is entitled to their own personal decisions. My only intention is to bring awareness to the emphasis placed upon wearing your hair texture in a permanently straightened hairstyle religiously.

I desire to highlight the way many individuals in the black community use this process as a means of identification and I want to reverse that mindset to begin cultivating self-acceptance of an organic nature.

The rejection of self does not manifest by simply placing a chemical on your head or even wearing someone else's hair for that matter. It begins by thinking that this process is what creates beauty, acceptance, respect, and prosperity. I want to help enable you to feel proud of who you are genuinely. I need you to know that you are naturally *more* than enough.

I not only speak from research and education, but from my own personal experiences. I was once the girl sitting in the professional stylist's chair, lying to her when she asked if I was "burning" because I didn't want her to rinse my relaxer out for fear that it wasn't straight enough. I wore weaves for so long that when I finally decided to stop, people were amazed that I had "cut off all of that long pretty hair." I endured chemical burns to my scalp on so many occasions that the sensation of feeling "pins and needles" had become normal to me during the process of relaxing my hair. I spent a countless amount of money on hair that was mine simply because "I'd bought it."

Whenever I caught a glimpse of myself in the mirror needing a "touch up" or a fresh weave, I felt ugly, naked, and insecure. I was defined by my hair and now, looking back on this process, I see it as such a tortuous event. But during that season of my life, I didn't care because I endured every aspect of that routine all in the name of beauty.

When I finally made the decision to embrace my return natural, the reactions that I received were a mixture of motivating, shocking, hurtful, and humorous.

I loved hearing things like "You're rocking that cut, girl!" and "Your hair really brings out your natural beauty." But unfortunately for me, it appeared that the bad was outweighing the good and the majority of comments I received were mostly negative. I heard things like:

❖ "Honey, are you going through some-thing?"

❖ "Yeah, this is temporary. You'll be getting a relaxer real soon!"

❖ "Sooooo, you're not going to keep it like that,

are you?"

❖ "Oh, it's not as nappy as I thought it would be! It's actually really soft!"

❖ "There's just other hairstyles I prefer on a woman. That nappy stuff ain't one of them!"

❖ "Nikki…What the hell?!?!"

❖ (*And this one is my personal favorite and most memorable*) "Are you Muslim now?"

People were acting as if I'd decided to paint myself blue and live like an extraterrestrial being. My family and closest friends were certain that I'd relax my hair again. They labeled it a phase and said I'd outgrow it. At that time, I wasn't quite sure where this natural hair journey would lead me, but one thing I knew for sure was that I was completely and totally done with chemically processing my hair.

I can vividly remember the first time I decided to get my kinky head of hair styled at a professional hair salon. I was still new on this hair journey, so I had very little knowledge of natural hair salons or even confidence in my own ability to care for my hair. My only knowledge of a professional salon was the setting that I worked in for so many years as a shampoo assistant/apprentice, so I booked an appointment just like I'd always done in the past.

When I arrived and sat in the chair, the stylist held no reservation in voicing her opinion about the things I should consider in making my hair "more manageable." After an extremely uncomfortable shampoo session, I sat up to reveal my shrunken Afro to a salon of naysayers. It seemed like the entire salon fell silent as I sat in the styling chair and removed the towel from my head.

I looked up and caught the stare of an old friend waiting for a haircut. He made an "Ew, yuck" face and shook his head from left to right slowly. I felt horrible. I was embarrassed.

I wanted to grab my stuff and run out of the door. But I stayed and waited while the stylist tried to figure out what to do. She eventually combed it out, blow dried it, and said, "I'll just press it and figure out what to do from there." How convenient.

Why was I going through all of this in a placed filled with people who looked just like me? Did they not know that the hair they were frowning upon was similar to that of their own? Did they not know that this was how my hair grew from my head naturally? Why were they acting as if my hair was a contagious disease?!

"This is black hair, dammit! Embrace it!" I wanted to scream so badly.

Centuries of thought manipulation has left us unaware of the need to facilitate self acceptance. So many of us don't even realize the pain we're constantly inflicting upon ourselves and upon others. We actively embrace and accept the rejection of our very existence, while making and agreeing with remarks that clearly highlight this negative thinking amongst our own.

- ❖ "I don't have the face to go natural."

- ❖ "Natural isn't for everyone."

- ❖ "See, you can go natural because you have that good hair!"

- ❖ "If I went natural, I'd look like a slave."

We do this without thinking twice about the generational curses that this type of mentality fundamentally creates.

Through unveiling the truth about our history, our people and our society, we can begin to establish a sense of pride in our heritage. And through that interaction, we can embrace our natural beauty with poise.

ENCOURAGING RECONNECTION

Canceling a negative thought requires you to replace it with a positive one. Therefore we must eliminate the notion that our history began with slavery and begin to educate ourselves on the great ancestors who shined before that time. Doing so encourages a connection to our roots that will flourish with strength and pride.

Indeed, it is extremely necessary for us to connect with the beautiful starseeds who have previously paved the way for greatness. Reverencing influential pioneers like Harriet Tubman, Sojourner Truth and Ida B. Wells is a non-negotiable when connecting with our history. These women led movements during a time where advancement for individuals of African descent was unfathomable for most. Their legacies will live on triumphantly for generations to come.

But in order to fully reconnect with the royalty that flows through our veins, in order to grasp the authentic nature of our culture, we must reach back further into the boughs of our lineage and take hold of the greatness that lies there.

We must also reverence our ancestors like

Queen Hatshepsut, one of the only women chosen to reign as pharaoh over Egypt. Her legacy paints her as a powerful ruler who successfully built a wealthy country. We must honor and pay respect to women like Queen Nzinga, who fought against the Portuguese slave trade in Africa while establishing respect for her authority as queen for the Mbundu people in (what we now know as) Angola . We must take pride in knowing that our people were the masterminds behind medicine, science, astrology, mathematics, language, art and musical instruments. We must take the initiative to open books, learn from others, and educate ourselves on those great individuals who we've never even heard of. This is where our history begins. This is who we are.

There have been movies, stories, and religions crafted after the true history of our people, but in an effort to keep us ignorant of our royal lineage, we've yet to get recognition that these people did indeed look like us.

To know and connect with our original history allows us to not only understand ourselves better, but it allows us to fully understand the world around us and operate effectively in the society that we live in today. Knowing that we come from greatness beyond what we've ever known gives us an immeasurable sense of pride and an elevated knowledge of self worth.

Take, for instance, a place in time where that essence of authentic history fueled the black community. During the late 1960s to 1970s, our community understood the authority that ran through their veins. Being black was a movement! Natural hair represented beauty and we, as a culture, embraced that.

During that era, natural hair was the norm. Black people from all walks of life connected with the spirit of their natural appearance and considered it acceptable. They redefined what beauty was in relation to people of African descent. For them, the nappy roots of an Afro and curly strands of "big hair" stood for more than a fashion statement. It delivered a message that let the world know they existed.

Television shows, magazine advertisements, commercials, musicians, athletes, models and activists all filled the air with soulful energy and dignified vibrations. They stood on their funky platform shoes while letting their hair stretch high into the universe. They were a walking symbol of consciousness, awareness, and value.

We must recreate that era. We must get back to that type of acceptance and partner it with implementations for change. And once we return, we must remain in that space.

This is how we create our own standards of beauty. This is how we connect to the electric energy that resides within the uniqueness of our genetics. It's time to manifest a permanent shifting that proves favorable to our community. It's time for a new revolution!

Nubian Goddess of natural beauty, allow your spirit to shine bright and illuminate your very existence. Allow the divine energy within to greet the eyes of man. Beauty begins within.

Luhv

Bronzed skin bathed by the element of light.

Mountainous curves of glory.

Anointed peaks and sanctified valleys.

Walking in the essence of a Goddess.

Luhv is her aroma.

Kinks and coils reaching for the celestial realm.

The color of darkness.

All-powerful imagery and heavenly perceptions.

Head held high like a Queen.

Luhv is her essence.

Brown eyes telling an immaculate story.

A soul of supremacy.

Hypnotizing potency and omnipotent energy.

Gazing through a quartz. The crystal is clear.

Luhv is her guide.

The flow caressing ears with sweet fruits.

A full portal of precision.

Supernatural interpretations and elevated vibrations.

Prophesying a message of exaltation.

Luhv is her truth.

Ready for war.

Overpowering oppression.

Vanquishing doubt.

Honor. Pride. Respect.

Luhv is her weapon.

THE HEALING PROCESS OF
BLACK HAIR

THOUGHTS WITHIN OUR COMMUNITY

When we come to understand our innate ability to be great, we will also come to understand and acknowledge the need for a healing process to begin within our community. Without a complete mental shift, we are unable to transcend to our highest level of self.

I took some time to ask random people one purposely vague question: "What do you think about natural hair in the black community?" Many gave their honest opinions in response to the question. Some were in favor of wearing natural hair and showed pride in voicing their opinion. Others were against it and weren't afraid to say so. Some people seemed to craft their answer in a way that they thought would be less offensive to me, a natural-haired woman in the black community. Others declined to answer all together. (All statements have been published anonymously to protect the innocent).

❖ Male, 24: "It's cool as long as she doesn't keep it
like that forever."

❖ Male, 35: "It's all over the place. Black people need to embrace their natural beauty, their essence, and love themselves unconditionally and let their beauty shine from the inside out."

❖ Female, 26: "I wish it was okay for corporate America. I'm a supervisor. I can't go natural. My manager would look at me like I was crazy!"

❖ Female, 30+: "I love my natural hair. I think more women should embrace it and stop trying to spend so much money buying hair that's the opposite texture."

❖ Female, 40+: "Truly, and this is my personal opinion, I don't think there's any excuse for anyone to be walking around with nappy hair nowadays."

❖ Female, 30+: "I like it, but my boyfriend hates it. He wants me to look pretty all the time so I keep the weaves for him."

❖ Male, 40+: "It's a lost trade. It's also overlooked as the way to go for our women."

❖ Female 50+: "Younger women need to know that their hair is their crown. It represents royalty and who they are as black women."

❖ Female, 6: "I think it's cute and it's, well, you know, beautiful. And it's life."

❖ Female, 5: "Um, that's pretty hard. Locs are cool. Black hair is cool. Brown hair is cool. Even if you have puffy hair, you can do anything you want. You can still do it."

❖ Male, 41: "I think it's up to the individual. I don't think that wearing natural hair makes you any more or any less ethnic! Chemically [processed] hair is a good choice and looks very good on some. However you can be natural and still pressed. It's up to the individual and their preference."

❖ Male, 30+: "Natural hair ain't for everybody, but a lot of times I feel that way is because some folks don't know how to make it look nice especially in the short-ugly phase. I love natural hair when it's longer and it's styled nice. I've noticed for me, and I'm sure others feel the same, that I tend to respect those who grow their natural hair long and takes care of it more than I do a women that has processed hair. It says a lot about that person's character without me ever talking to them. It says that this person is patient, takes care of herself, and doesn't worry what people think because they had to go through the ugly phase."

❖ Male, 29: "I love natural hair in the black community as long as it's taken care of and looks nice. I've seen the good natural hairstyles and I've also seen the not so good ones. All in all, I would like to see more well taken care of natural styles [to] keep us connected to our roots."

❖ Female 30+: "Well, I am a newbie. I am still searching for the right look for me on this natural journey. I'm glad to have a supportive husband who keeps me encouraged. I briefly thought about joining the creamy crack family again, but came to my senses. The fact that it is not accepted has had my mind in a world wind. I am searching and trying new things that fit me. Tried the tiny Afro look and that just was not for me. It was a part of this journey I had to go through though."

❖ Female 30+: "I'm against it for myself. My hair is too thick and it requires time. That's great for those of you that have a natural and keep it looking good.

❖ Female 30+: "I think, as a cosmetologist, it's beautiful. I'm natural for the fifth time, and the longest time. Before, I would go back to relaxers only because there was very little info about how to take care of your natural locks properly. I have very tight coils and I now embrace them. It's still a lot of work but so is relaxed hair."

❖ Male,7: "Huh? I don't know. It's nice, I guess." (*laughs*)

❖ Female, 8: "Sometimes I like to wear my hair straight because the girls in my class have their hair long and straight. But mine is always frizzy
when I wear it down. So I just like when my mom does braids. I really like beads, too."

Evidently, there is a wide range of opinions. While this is to be expected, I call it unacceptable. When looking at these responses, what can we conclude?

❖ That some young girls are being taught to love their natural hair while others are continuing to have media, society, and peers mold their perceptions.

❖ That many desire to reconnect with their natural essence, but feel more comfortable with allowing European standards of beauty to define them.

❖ That some men have elevated their consciousness enough to accept the natural beauty that is the black woman in every aspect of her glory.

❖ That many men think that they are embracing the natural beauty of black
   women, but are still (sometimes subconsciously) judging that image based on
   European standards.

❖ That others have yet to understand the
   beauty that is natural hair and continue to
   allow false images, facades, and perceptions to shape their mentality.

❖ That if we begin with the youth, who gen-
   erally have no initial perception of beauty
   standards, their mentality can be shifted to
   favor acceptance and self-love.

Out of all of the conclusions that can be
drawn, the most important, and possibly overlooked one, is that black hair in its' natural state
is not the "norm."

This shows that there is a great work to be
done from within. If natural hair was the norm ,
we'd all be comfortable with the organic nature
of black beauty and there would be no reason to
question its presence.

We cannot expect others to take our need for
acceptance seriously if we aren't thinking on the
same level about the standards of beauty for our

own people.

Many of us are feeling the pull to participate in this movement. We want to return. We want to redefine standards for our children and their children. But because we are not operating on one accord regarding the beauty standards for black women, we allow doubt, fear, and uncertainty to creep in and deter us from the image we so badly wish to embrace. *Will "he" like it? What will my boss think? How will I get through the "ugly" phase? Am I still pretty? Does this "fit my face"? Am I fierce? Is this jazzy? Do I look militant?*

We feel this strong urge from deep within to embrace ourselves naturally, but years of thought manipulation has created a battleground for this process. We fight with ourselves when there should be no need to do so. There should be no hesitation once you've decided to return natural. We should not feel uneasy about wanting to bask in the way we were uniquely created. But unfortunately, we've been the victim of a big societal bully and we are now left with unhealed wounds that create uncertainty.

Though many of us may not realize it, we are operating daily with holistic wounds that have been open for quite some time; most of which we incurred during early childhood. We have passed down the mindsets and thought patterns of those wounds to our children and for some, our grand-children. We are refusing to exercise, have fun, and enjoy certain adventures that increase the vitality of life because we don't want to mess up our hair. We are constantly praising "good hair" and making that old rambunctious "bad hair" sit still in a corner. We do all of this simply because we feel doubt about our appearance as naturals.

For some of us, a return comes with a list of strict stipulations. We like natural hair, but only if it lays a certain way on our shoulders. We approve of natural hair, but only when it's a particular texture. We are the ones who believe that natural hair can only be worn by a chosen few. We are the ones who embrace the curls, but banish the kinks and coils.

This conversation with a recently transitioned natural lends a great example:

> **Her:** I want you to take a look at my friend's hair. She needs help! She wants to go natural, but she can't do that.
>
> **Me:** (*laughs*) What? Why not?
>
> **Her:** Girl, she don't have good hair like that!

Me: Please stop it.

Her: What? She don't.

Me: What is good hair?

Her: C'mon, you know what good hair is.

Me: No, I don't. Really, what is it?

Her: I'm not trying to say it has to be like white people's hair or anything, but you know, like see? (*She starts running her fingers through her hair*.) I can play with my curls easily. She can't do that. It's all damaged and uneven and it looks like she just needs to cut it all off and start over or something.

Me: Oh, her hair is damaged. Let's say that her hair needs a bit of love and care to restore it to a healthy state naturally, but let's not use the term "good hair" anymore, ever again, in this lifetime, or the next one. Okay?

Her: (*smiles slightly*) Okay.

Or take for example a public conversation between two beautiful black women regarding one's personal hair journey.

Woman 1: (In reference to a picture of herself that showcases her straightened, mid-length hair) I have to give a major shout out to my hair stylist. She has my hair laid! All-natural black girl with white girl hair. No tracks!

Woman 2: Oh no, honey! It's still black girl hair; it's just that *good* black girl hair!

Now did these women have good intentions on embracing their return? Yes, I'm almost positive that they did. The young lady that I was speaking with seemed to genuinely want help for her friend's hair. And "Woman Two" gave a grand attempt at trying to encourage her friend to love her "black girl hair." The problem occurs when each woman labeled a certain image as "good." Both comments signal the misconceptions and ignorant perceptions that continually circulate amongst our people.

Thus it is pertinent to take a moment and address this ideology in particular. We'll begin again with another elementary-based lesson of definition.

Good (adjective): Of high quality; correct or proper.

Bad (adjective): Low or poor in quality, not correct or proper; not pleasant, pleasing, or enjoyable.

The use of these words in relation to the description of black hair is not only a blatant act of division within our own community, but it is the very thinking that keeps us stagnant. This particular mentality makes it almost impossible for us, as a unit, to redefine the standards of beauty for people of African descent. "Good hair" does *not* exist! To believe so implies that anything other than that which you deem as "good" is ultimately bad. By utilizing the "good hair" description, you're essentially labeling other various types and textures "poor in quality."

If you're guilty of this thinking, from this day forward, vow that you will remove that notion from your mentality entirely. To begin healing, we have to treat those wounds that have been infected for far too long. "Good hair" versus "bad hair" is to growth in the black community as dirt is to a cut in human flesh. They are both counter-productive to the healing process and should thus be avoided at all costs.

In most cases, the classification of good versus bad stems from texture and type. Hair *textures* can be fine, medium, and thick, while hair *types* can be straight, wavy, curly, and kinky-curly (or what some call "coily"). These terms are of great use to individuals in the field of cosmetology and hair care. They are also great for your personal journey and help you gain a full knowledge of how to properly care for your individual head of hair. They are not, however, useful in grading individuals with labels of good and bad. No one texture or type is better than another. That thought is poison to your entire lineage of existence. You are who you are. Your hair is what it is. There is no right, wrong, good, bad, pretty, or ugly spectrum. It is all good in the sight of authentic creation and accepting that truth allows for an enjoyable journey as you return.

For many women in the black community, the negative mindsets aforementioned make the process of "going natural" a daunting task. They've added a section for hair products in their neatly organized spending plans so that they can look forward to purchasing every product that promises them the perfect curls. They constantly try different techniques and styles to get their hair to look like their favorite big-haired celebrity idol, to no avail. And before long, they're yelling out "I can't do this," because the creamy crack is calling their name.

What these women don't realize is that

they've set themselves up for failure. They were defeated before they began their journey. They "went natural" with the image of their favorite curly haired crush glued in their mind, only she was wearing a face that looked like their very own. And when that fabricated image failed to become reality, disappointment set in and they came to believe that "being natural isn't for everyone."

Embracing the mindset of returning natural promotes self-acceptance, self-love, and self-respect. You'll embrace *your* individual texture, whatever it may be. And while admiring the beauty of others, you'll know and understand your own beauty in a more authentic light. You won't "feel ugly" as your teeny afro grows with much personality. You won't exert an enormous amount of energy into trying to make your thick, curly hair appear less frizzy and more tamed. You won't require a lengthy transition to embrace your return.

You'll be confident in your spirit-led choice to return natural and you'll do it with elegance. You will walk with your head held high and exude an astronomical amount of confidence.

To comprehend this concept is to further advance the movement of returning natural for black women all over the globe. Embracing your history and genuinely loving your natural image will allow your hair to symbolize a historical transformation as opposed to another small stamp in time.

A SHIFT IN MENTALITY

Why is this even important? Why does it matter? The answer to those questions and thoughts are summed up with two words: *Our future*.

It matters because there is a generation of black youth who are being raised in a society that constantly devalues their image. Everywhere they turn, they are told that they aren't enough as they naturally are, whether it's mass media, society and sometimes even through us! Yes, we are responsible for delivering that same message of inferiority to our youth.

- ❖ Infants are losing their hairlines before their first birthday, because we're so pressed to pull their hair up into tight hairstyles and put heavy bows on it to make it "look pretty," instead of allowing it to be free and innocent just as they are.
- ❖ Three-year-olds are getting extensions simply because Mommy wants their braids to be "long and pretty."
- ❖ Four-year-olds are crying in the salon because the chemical on their head is literally eating away at their flesh, yet

they are being told that it's okay because "beauty is pain." They are then being asked if they want to "be pretty or not" as a means to quiet them down as they endure the torturous procedure.

❖ Ten-year-olds are wearing full weave installations with ringlets curled to look exactly like popular reality TV stars and thinking it's good to be "bad."

All of these actions encourage our young princesses to grow up and disown their royal bloodline. They aren't concerned with operating as Queens because they're all too busy trying to place a value on their existence that can be measured.

To institute a change in the mentality of our community, we must change our actions and thought patterns with our future generations in mind. We must begin to encourage self-acceptance early in their journey of life.

If we take a moment and watch the shows that they are enticed to watch on every kid-friendly television channel, look at the images covering the pages of their storybooks, and observe the toys stocked high on the shelves of their favorite store, we'll notice the need to take an extra step in enforcing their own image as beautiful.

It is apparent that, just like our generation, they are being molded to believe that their natural beauty is secondary. Although some companies are beginning to incorporate very small examples to combat this thought, it's simply just not enough. There aren't enough dolls with afros, storybook princesses with curly hair, or television stars with locs. If we don't make a greater effort to highlight this as an issue, the intended cycle of destruction will continue. We will continue to question our natural beauty and battle with its acceptance.

Some feel that we are leading the way for this change by defying the current norm and embracing a natural return. But, unfortunately, we aren't delving deep enough into the realms of ancient understanding and teaching lessons to ignite a fire burning with pride and value.

Wearing our natural hair in a sleek puff and wearing Ankh-shaped earrings is not enough to show our young children the way toward self-enlightenment. We must put forth a physical, mental, and metaphysical effort to educate them. We must elevate them through knowledge. We must show them that, by understanding their roots, embracing their stolen culture, and walking in their divine authority, they can and will institute change.

Take them to events. Watch documentaries. Read books to them. Have fun with sharing knowledge and encouraging their self-acceptance. Be mindful of the need to create balance within their world and don't be afraid to implement that change.

Consciously praise the organic beauty of your young princess regularly. Let her be free to rock her natural hair with pride. Don't be afraid to incorporate books with black characters, by black authors, into her library of popular princesses with long blonde hair.

Encourage her to watch independent films and cartoons that exemplify her heritage. Let her know that she is perfect in her own right. Encourage her self-worth and allow her to experience the power of becoming secure in her own skin.

Allow your young prince to acknowledge and embrace the beauty that rests within our natural appearance. Give him images that encourage him to accept the women of his community just as they are. Combat the imagery that tells him what he should consider as beautiful and allow him to know the royal essence of his culture. Help him appreciate the authenticity of a black hair.

By doing this, you not only create a shift in mentality, but you foster a healing for our community that will continue throughout generations to come. That shift possesses the power to redefine the standards of beauty in our community. Although that type of change requires time, it is definitely attainable.

To institute a shift of that magnitude, you must begin within self. If we all become accountable for our own thoughts and begin to embrace natural hair as an individual movement first, we can then begin to institute that same movement globally. We can implement a real change.

NIKKI'S NATURALS

As a holistic hair care consultant and natural hair transition coach, I've encountered many questions about the process of returning natural and ways to embrace the journey. Some of the questions that come are individual specific, yet I've found that numerous questions appear to be very similar in nature. This tells me that there are many women who have the same questions, comments and concerns regarding their natural hair journey.

Here are the top six most common and memorable comments that I've encountered. Through these few concerns, I've been able to engage in conversations that not only educates, but inspires and uplifts Queens from all walks of life.

1. I want to do a big chop but I'm nervous about cutting all of my hair off.

- Being nervous about change is a normal reaction. It doesn't mean that you shouldn't do it, it just means that you should be gentle with yourself as you begin the journey and know that it will take you a moment to get used to seeing beauty in a different light. Cut it with confidence! Take yourself on a shopping spree for new earrings, grab a couple of vibrant lipstick shades and shine bright Super (si)Star!

2. I'm finally happy with my natural hair and now I want to embrace my grey hair, but I'm not sure if I can handle that transition.

- The same feelings you worked through while embracing your natural hair journey are similar to the feelings that you work through while embracing your natural hair color. The key to making it easier this time around is realizing that you've done it before so you should be a pro this time around. You already know that it's a journey because as your hair goes through changes, you will too. But you also know that, eventually, you will grow deeply in love with your new look. You know that you'll soon radiate confidence and empower others to embrace their journey. You know that YOU'VE GOT THIS! So don't sweat it.

3. I wish I could get locks, but they're not professional enough for my career.

- Any natural hairstyle, be it locked or loose, is professional enough for any career choice (even the ones who have written rules in their conduct books against them). The issue occurs when we support the idea that our natural hair is, indeed, unsuitable for certain situations. Yes, I agree that unruly/unkept hair is not appropriate for a professional or corporate environment; but that generalization does not instantly include locks, braids, twists, afros etc. If your hair is clean, neat and subtly styled or colored, I dare to say that it IS professional enough for your career. Education around the different processes for locking your hair and understanding your options for styling can help bring peace to your desire to begin the journey. Lock it. Load it. And Love it!

4. My hair is taking forever to grow.

- Watching you hair grow is the equivalent to the entertaining event of watching grass grow. The more you check on it, the less it appears to grow. Ignore the height of the grass as you move throughout your days and before you know it, your yard is looking like it belongs in the everglades. Daily length checks will keep you feeling like your hair isn't growing as quickly as you feel it should. Focus on nurturing the strands with love and relieve the stress of growth. Before you know it, you'll have hair growth and retention that confirms that this natural hair journey was the best decision for your holistic beauty experience.

5. Let's straighten it today; I want to look really pretty!

- When we use straight hair to define pretty, we subconsciously continue to support the idea that our natural hair texture is the opposite. I am not saying that it is wrong to create change. I am saying that it is wrong to define that change as something better. Only straightening our hair to celebrate a holiday, attend a special event," feel pretty" or put our best foot forward simply says one thing aloud, "YOU ARE NOT ENOUGH AS YOU ARE NATURALLY CREATED". Try a new natural updo when your womanly essence is in need of a boost. Add some hair jewelry to celebrate a holiday. Give your daughter a beautiful head of roller set curls to accompany her ensemble for a special event. Your natural is pretty enough for any special moment within your life.

6. I'm about to relax this mess! I can't do this anymore. It's just too nappy!

- Many women quit the journey before it ever truly begins. Mentality is the key contributing factor to this issue. We give the word "nappy" a derogatory connotation. We label our kinks and coils as "mess", "crap" and "junk". If this type of energy was being pored into me, I'm sure I'd be unable to flourish beautifully as well. Let's get Happy to be Nappy! Let's love our hair and give it time to show us how powerful its presence truly is. When you've been manipulating chemically straightened hair or weaving extensions for decades, learning to care for your naturally tight curl pattern may lend a learning curve that requires patience. It wont all happen overnight, but it will happen. Just give it time and be open to obtaining the knowledge needed to care for your coils with love and pride.

No matter what your concerns are along this journey, it is extremely important to always remember that where attention goes, energy flows. Be confident in your choice to return natural. Feel the beauty of every step this transformation brings. Radiate the light that warms from within and glow with self-love. If you embrace "You", then others will too!

INSPIRING CHANGE

When we've connected to the essence of our roots and have come to fully understand the society that we live in, we will then begin to inspire a new generation. We'll look far beyond the perfect natural hairstyle and see the perfect natural beauty. We will come to understand the fact that who we are as a people is organically enough. And even if we choose to foster a change through experimenting with different hairstyles, we'll utilize them as an extra measure to the things we do as women and not use them as a cover up for who we are afraid to be naturally.

When we have researched and discovered that the truth within our history reaches far beyond the torment of our ancestors, when we have acknowledged our wounds and have begun to facilitate healing, when we can standup individually and say "Hey, this is me and I love it" without reprise, we will effectively ignite a flame that inspires a change for our entire community.

As simplistic as it may seem, one great way to inspire change is by giving compliments. Sometimes, all we need is the "go-ahead" from another sister or brother in the community to keep us encouraged as we boldly embrace our return.

Take, for instance, the following example. I was wandering around a parking lot late one evening, searching for my car and I heard the engine of a large pickup truck creeping up behind me.

"Excuse me," said the middle-aged brother from behind the wheel. I kept walking as if I didn't hear him. I didn't want to slow down until I reached my car.

"I'm sorry. Excuse me, ma'am," he said with a slight elevation in his tone.

I stopped and turned around.

Yes," I said, forcing a smile though my concerned facial expression.

"I just wanted to stop and say that I noticed you were wearing your hair natural," he said sincerely. "It looks really good on you and I think you should keep it that way. That's all. I just wanted to pay you that compliment."

I was shocked.

"Wow, well, thank you. I appreciate that," I replied.

"Have a great evening," he said with a smile

and drove away.

I had not done anything special to my hair on that day. It was a simple "wash and go" type of day. But the fact that this King took the time to stop and compliment me set off a light bulb.

What if more men did this within our community? What if more Queens got honest compliments from Kings praising their natural beauty and encouraging them to embrace it? Would we feel more empowered? Would we be less reluctant to embrace our transition? Would we feel more confident?

And what if, as we grow deeper in love with ourselves naturally, we began to compliment our sisters regularly? Would it inspire unity? Would it build our esteem collectively? Would we grow together and reclaim our thrones as beautiful Queens of color?

To see significant results, each individual must accept the charge to love and be loved. We must show the world that our hair and indigenous beauty are sacred images that possess a powerful message.

Knowing this and remaining steadfast in the journey to embrace and empower the return will make black hair, in its natural state, a more acceptable and appreciated form of beauty in our community.

However, it is important to note that we cannot wait on society or individuals of other communities to lend their stamp of approval for this transition. If we do, it will never occur. Whether fear of dominance, ignorance, lack of empathy or merely being unconcerned, many factors can play into why others may never take the initiative to endorse this movement. For that reason, it is up to us and only us, to proudly stand up and redefine our own standards.

To ensure that there are no misconceptions or uncertainty in regard to the things that we can do to promote accountability within this process, next you will find 10 activities to help foster change. Implementing these actions within your circle of family and friends will facilitate healing within the black community regarding natural hair and thus render your contribution to redefining societal norms.

TEN ACTIVITIES FOR HEALING

Activity 1 – Movie Night

Have a movie night with your family and watch a documentary on the history of people of African descent. Make sure that it is one that authentically includes indigenous cultural practices, royal figures, and the supreme intelligence of our people.

Have a film discussion.

1. Were you surprised by the information?
2. How did you feel before, during, and after the film?
3. How can you apply what you learned to your life today?

NOTES:

_____

_____

_____

_____

_____

_____

_____

Activity 2 – Write a Research Paper

We've all written research papers for a school assignments or work project, but how many of us actually apply that activity to our personal lives? Do you remember how much information you uncovered while writing a research paper? You may have started off completely clueless, but after researching and writing, you were knowledgeable enough to provide pertinent information regarding your topic.

Pick a topic regarding the beauty images of black women, black hair, hairstyles or products, and write a research paper on it. Get your family involved. Have everyone write his or her paper throughout the month and at the end of the month, prepare a nice in-home event where everyone can share and discuss his or her findings over a huge feast.

NOTES:

_____

_____

_____

_____

_____

_____

_____

Activity 3 – Take a Trip

Sometimes you have to travel to learn more about your history. Black history museums and memorial structures are all over the world. You might even find one in your hometown or a surrounding area. Additionally you can plan a trip and travel abroad to connect with authentic cultures. Talk to the residents of the areas. Connect with the elders. Obtain knowledge about a specific time from the experiences of others. Take what you've learned and use your own personal research to dig deeper into that history.

1. What else can you uncover?

2. How can you apply that information to your journey as you return natural?

3. What did you find that encouraged, empowered, or inspired you?

NOTES:

_____

_____

_____

_____

_____

_____

_____

Activity 4 – Read

Do what was once illegal for many of our ancestors . The more you read, the more you know. Begin building a large library filled with information on your cultural identity. Find truths to combat the lies and myths that we've been fed throughout the years. By gaining knowledge, you can discover a completely new world where your pride in your culture is paramount.

NOTES:

_____

_____

_____

_____

_____

_____

_____

Activity 5 – Start a Natural Hair Club

❖ Get a few of your family members, close friends, co-workers, and neighbors together and begin connecting monthly.

❖ Make sure everyone is already natural, transitioning, or interested in returning.

❖ Do activities 1-4 as a group or just get together and discuss questions, encounters, and emotions surrounding your return.

❖ Plan club meetings and have fun while you share knowledge.

There's nothing more aesthetically pleasing than a group of black women, all different shades and sizes with all different textures and types of natural hair, looking gorgeous while vibrating love energy. That presence is an undeniable power filled with beauty.

NOTES:

_____

_____

_____

_____

_____

_____

_____

Activity 6 – Support Other Naturals

- ❖ Purchase homemade hair products, T-shirts, hair accessories, books, and other items from independent black-owned companies that support the return.
- ❖ Share the products with others in the community and encourage them to support black businesses as well.
- ❖ Begin circulating money within the black community while promoting our positive self-images.

NOTES:

_____
_____
_____
_____
_____
_____
_____

Activity 7 – Affirm daily

Speak the below affirmation daily. Scream it at the top of your lungs. Let the Universe know your intentions.

I embrace the beauty that is naturally me.

My crown emits powerful love energy.

I am confident.

I am proud.

I am bold in my royal essence.

I shine bright from within.

I am naturally beautiful.

Write your own affirmation and commit it to memory for daily use.

NOTES:

_____

_____

_____

_____

_____

_____

_____

Activity 8 – Attend a Natural Hair Event

❖ Find an event promoting natural hair and holistic health in your area and make plans to attend. Share the event with others and encourage them to attend as well.

❖ Network with pioneers in the natural hair care industry to help build your knowledge of black hair.

❖ Take advantage of the vast amount of information available to you in one location.

NOTES:

_____
_____
_____
_____
_____
_____
_____

Activity 9 – Start a Blog

Start a written or video blog that documents your return.

❖ Take photos of your hair throughout the journey.
❖ Express your feelings and experiences.
❖ Share the knowledge that you're learning with others and help someone else along their journey.
❖ Inspire women to return natural and encourage society to embrace that return.
❖ Stimulate dialogue and empower your fellow sisters.

NOTES:

_____

_____

_____

_____

_____

_____

_____

Activity 10 – Love Your Return

Let the passion for your return shine bright. Consciously rock your afro, locs, kinks, and curls with pride. Set the example for others to follow by telling the world that you love who you are authentically. By exuding confidence, you can inspire both men and women to connect with your royal beauty.

NOTES:

_____

_____

_____

_____

_____

_____

_____

More and more women are embracing their return, and as this movement continues to occur, we all have an individual responsibility to promote awareness. We must wake up and spread the knowledge that we uncover through our own private transition. We must take a stand, one by one, and redefine what society tells us we should look like in order to advance, succeed, and possess a title of beauty. Through connecting with the legacy of your ancestors, understanding your culture, elevating in consciousness, acknowledging the need for healing and putting forth a genuine effort to promote the required antidote, you can empower others with the substance of your personal journey.

All that we need, [nature] gives to us. She's generous and we can trust her.

Momma Nature

Her whispers deliver a message of friendship. Her touch is soothing. Her presence is refreshing. I allow her to caress my soul.

Because of her, I breathe.

Her calmness is relaxing. An encounter with her brings new life. Her supernatural powers strip away any carnal filth and I'm left feeling rejuvenated.

Because of her, I am.

The passion that fuels her light to shine bright energizes me. She's vibrant. She lifts me up, whenever I'm down. She kisses me and I glow.

Because of her, I live.

Her gifts are bountiful. She never stops giving. She nourishes my spirit. She heals me. She says eat and I do. She says drink, and I do. She loves in vivid color and because of her, I grow.

I sit with her. I walk with her. I talk to her. I connect with her. And then, I transcend.

THE HOLISTIC HEALTH OF
BLACK HAIR

What is (w)Holism?

The concept of (w)holism (used inter-changeably with holism) is one that, when under-stood and applied, can impact your life in a way that delivers success on many levels. (W)holism focuses on our entire existence as one unit. In-stead of treating the mind, body and spirit as in-dividual parts, we treat them as the whole in an effort to create balance and eliminate dis-ease. Focusing on the whole person reminds us to take into account the mental, physical and emotional components of our individual selves when seek-ing to promote wellness.

This practice is widely used to heal ailments and dis-ease within the body, bring peace to our mental capacities and provide supernatural eleva-tion to our spirits. Through holism, we come to know the ultimate meaning of life. We come to know love, peace, joy, and happiness.

Returning natural is about more than simply cutting the relaxed hair off your head. It's a com-plete shift in consciousness and lifestyle habits. Although you may not have realized it, holistic health plays a major role in the condition of your hair. From moisture retention to growth, all of the components of your hair are affected if there is an imbalance present within the whole unit. Our hair follicles contain some of the most rapidly growing cells within the body, so when we are out of balance and experiencing dis-ease, our hair will internalize that imbalance and react by slowing the production of healthy and vibrant hair strands. Therefore, it is necessary to incorporate holistic health practices into your hair care routine.

MIND AND HAIR

Your mind is the battlefield where life plays itself out. Therefore, your thoughts have a major role in creating a healthy environment for hair growth.

We incur thousands of thoughts daily and many of us have yet to master the strategy of controlling those thoughts and using them to our benefit. Because of this, many of us create stress, tension, and complications within ourselves. We over think things that are beyond our control. We try to figure out every detail of every encounter.

Some of us have learned to control negativity, but we've yet to learn how to use our thoughts to create our ideal lives. So we live a life of mediocrity while constantly desiring more. This too creates stressors.

Stress has been known to cause moderate-to-severe hair loss in many individuals. If you aren't controlling that aspect of your overall holistic health, you are inadvertently damaging your hair. Therefore, it is of the utmost importance that you are diligent in managing stress levels in an effort to maintain balance for impeccable health.

Here are three effective ways you can successfully master your thoughts, reduce stress, and cultivate balance.

Acknowledge The Positive:

It's so easy to dwell on the negative things happening all around us and within our world. You can constantly look at what's wrong and complain about those things. You can choose to allow uncontrollable situations to create havoc and run rampant throughout your thoughts or you can choose to think positively. This takes some time and practice, but it is a skill that must be mastered in order to establish a holistically healthy lifestyle. To begin this practice you should:

1. **Start an "Attitude for Supreme Gratitude" journal.** This can be any type of journal or notebook. Simply commit to writing something new that you're grateful for on a daily basis. It can be something a large as your home or as small as your ability to purchase your favorite snack whenever you so desire. When you hear yourself complaining about all of the things that are going wrong in your life, whip out that journal and review the many things you

have to be grateful for. Another method is creating a "Just Thankful Jar." Write things that you're thankful for on note cards, place them in a jar, and put the jar in a common area of your home. Encourage your family members to get involved and whenever you're feeling ungrateful or negative, grab a note card out of the jar and read it. Be sure to replace a note card or two each time you make a withdrawal.

2. **Remain conscious of the amount of negativity you process.** When a negative thought arises, cancel it and replace it with a positive thought. For example, instead of thinking, "I hate going to work. My boss gets on my nerves," replace that thought with, "I'm thankful for all of the life lessons my job is teaching me. I'm learning how to interact with different personalities and that will be very useful when I start my own business."

You have to be conscious of even the smallest thoughts. If you wake up and stub your toe on the footboard of your bed, don't think, "Oh, no. This is going to be a bad day," because then it *will* be a bad day, simply because you thought it to be so. Stubbing your toe could mean that you need to rearrange your room for greater energy flow or that you need a new morning routine that doesn't leave you in a rush.

Consciously turning negative thoughts into positive ones requires a conscious effort, but eventually, it will become a habit.

Don't Worry About It:

Some things don't deserve the energy that we give them. Concerning yourself with every detail of every little situation creates stress. There are times when you just have to tell yourself that you're not going to worry about it, and then don't! Don't put energy into complaining, fussing, and elevating your vitals regarding every negative situation. Learn to just let things go and be at peace.

Unplug and Be Free:

There are also times when you may need to unplug to maintain your positivity. When you're feeling overwhelmed and managing stress becomes a struggle, unplug from it all. Retreat to nature and find serenity. Take a trip to the beach, rent a cabin in the mountains, or simply take a nice jog outdoors.

Breathing in fresh air and observing the beauty of nature calms the senses and clears the mind. Find something to do that requires nothing from you except for your ability to simply be free. This will inspire the balance you need to remain on track and keep your thoughts and actions clear of impurities.

By implementing a few strategies to help you remain positive, you can reduce the amounts of stress that you incur from simply living life. And as you control those levels, you create a vibrant environment that stimulates your body to perform effectively. You maintain happiness, improve health conditions, and consequently, you promote and retain hair growth and vitality.

BODY AND HAIR

Many people believe that healthy hair and growth retention comes from finding the best product to apply to their heads. And while stimulating the scalp and nurturing your follicles are great for the overall health of your hair, caring from the inside out is most beneficial. What you put *into* your body will always show on the outside. From your hair to your skin to your eyes and even your nails, if you aren't eating foods that provide true nourishment to your temple, it will show. For optimal holistic health and to encourage a beautiful head of healthy hair, you should:

1.   **Drink Water:** Drinking water hydrates your body and helps keep your hair and scalp moisturized.

2.   **Eat Whole Foods:** Fresh fruits and vegetables provide your hair with the necessary nutrients needed to thrive and remain healthy. Make sure you include enough protein and iron rich foods in your diet to facilitate hair growth and strength within the follicles.

3. **Juice:** Drinking fresh pressed juices will allow your body to obtain immediate nutrition and occasionally relieve your organs from the hard work of breaking down foods to obtain the antioxidants, vitamins, and minerals found in whole foods.

Healthy Hair Juice Recipe:

❖ 1 cup of Leafy Greens

❖ 1 (1-inch) piece of Ginger

❖ 3 Green Apples (cut in half)

❖ 1 Cucumber

❖ 1/2 Lemon (peeled)

Process ingredients through a juicer and enjoy!

This combination contains a substantial amount of minerals, silica, and zinc; all of which are needed to promote hair growth

Note: When purchasing whole foods, remember that organic produce is good and that locally grown is better. If you must purchase conventionally grown, be sure to wash your produce thoroughly as these fruits and vegetables are often times sprayed with pesticides to keep the bugs away during the growth process . You can do this by soaking the produce in a clean sink filled with 1 part vinegar and 3 parts water for 20 minutes and then rinsing clean.

4. **Enjoy Some Herbs:** Herbs like stinging nettle, burdock root, neem, and ginseng can be taken internally as a tea or used externally as rinses and treatments to prevent hair loss and stimulate growth.

5. **Get Your Vitamins:** The A, B-Complex, and C vitamins are all very essential to the health of your hair follicles. These vitamins can be obtained by eating various fruits, vegetables, whole grains, and some organic meats when prepared properly.

6. **Detox:** Although our body is designed to naturally detoxify itself, several life factors (contaminations in the air, water, and food) make it hard for this process to effectively occur. Giving your body a helping hand by only eating whole foods, drinking water, and cleansing your detox-

ification organs for a short period of time will help rid toxins that create dis-ease and prevent vitality.

7. **Exercise and Yoga:** Find an exercise routine that gets your heart pumping and your sweat rolling. The blood circulation and natural detoxification process of sweating helps to keep your body in good shape. Practicing yoga is a great way to build strength and flexibility while encouraging relaxation and establishing inner peace.

Anything other than nourishing your temple from within is only a temporary fix. Once you've created a thriving environment that radiates through to the outside, all of your topical product applications will act as an added benefit to the results of your healthy lifestyle, and thus create holistically healthy hair.

SPIRIT AND HAIR

Our hair grows in a way that symbolizes authority. It's big. It grows upward and outward. It hangs in a pattern that defies a uniformed structure. Our kinks and curls are leaders. They perform as they choose on many occasions. This demands respect and appreciation. Our hair represents our need to remain connected spiritually as we continue to operate within our supernatural power and authority.

Renewing ourselves daily and replenishing our spirits enables us to perform our tasks and complete our assignments of purpose here on earth. We receive confirmations, answers, and guidance for our journey through spirituality and through that connection, we can live happily and experience the goodness of life. When you're focused and living on purpose, your body is able to flourish in richness. You aren't overwhelmed by life's lessons. You aren't distracted by minuscule circumstances. You aren't creating a foundation built upon poison and asking your body to function fully and produce healthy hair, clear thinking, natural energy, or a supernatural understanding. You're operating in divine perfection, just as you should and allowing your life to unfold as it is so immaculately designed to do.

Prayer (talking) and meditation (listening) are the greatest factors in maintaining this connection. Many people are afraid of these practices or shy away from them because they aren't sure how to do them. In truth, there is no correct way to do them. It's a personal preference and a private journey. Sure, there are people who will try to tell you to begin with a certain phrase and end with a particular gesture. And yes, there are thousands of gurus chanting mantras over soft international melodies that guide you into a deep trance to clear your mind. But because we are all different, those concepts work for some and create ineffective experiences for others. Therefore, you should find what works best for you and incorporate that method into your holistic health lifestyle.

If listening to music with your eyes closed while lying in a tub of warm water elevates you to connection with a higher deity, do that. If lying on the ground and looking up at the sky connects you, do that. If sitting in complete silence and thinking about absolutely nothing delivers a supernatural experience, do that! Allow your spirit to lead you in meditation. Listen. Do what feels right to you.

Staying connected to the source will keep

you on target for fulfilling your destiny. Through living on purpose, you are able to enjoy life and experience bliss while here on earth. Living a life filled with love and remaining in tune spiritually generates great outcomes for your journey. Inner peace from spiritual elevation plays a major role in your holistic health lifestyle and should not be negotiated or neglected. Remain connected and live.

Balancing the mind, body, and spirit are vital to your overall health. These factors are key in allowing you to accomplish your assignment. You were created with a cause. Without living a lifestyle of (w)holism, it will be nearly impossible to successfully complete your mission.

Your health, from the kinks and curls atop your head to the pretty pedicure on your feet, should be balanced as one unit. Keeping your mind empowered, your body nurtured, and spirit renewed will allow you to walk in your true calling and authority as a descendant of royalty.

ALL-NATURAL HAIR CARE LOVE

When looking for products to incorporate into your hair care regimen, the options can become overwhelming. It seems that many manufacturers got the memo that black women were embracing their natural hair and now needed help with how to care for it. The same companies that you broke up with by ditching their boxed chemical products are now begging for you to come back to them and try their "natural hair" line. The problem with many of these companies is that they are still selling us things filled with chemicals and non-natural ingredients. They slapped the word "natural" on a label and placed a product on a shelf. But how helpful can a "natural" product be with limited "natural" ingredients?

There are three questions you can always ask yourself when searching out a new product to incorporate into your routine:

1. Did it take me longer than fifteen seconds to read the list of ingredients?

2. Is it hard for me to pronounce most of the major ingredients on the label?

3. Does this company manufacture other non-natural products?

If you answer yes to any of the above questions, that product may not be the best option for your return as it may contain many harsh and harmful ingredients.

There are some amazing products on the market that can work wonders for your natural hair and personal journey, but there are also just as many all-natural elixirs that you can whip up right in the privacy of your own home that are just as effective. Doing so will not only give you a peace about what's actually in the product, but it will enable your hair to experience a taste of the good life as well.

Eating clean foods, drinking water, and exercising allows life to thrive from within, but putting products made from all-natural ingredients on your hair, and even your skin, will partner with that effort and encourage a healthy grow and glow.

DIY ALL-NATURAL HAIR CARE PRODUCTS

The feeling of knowing every ingredient in your choice of beauty product is priceless. It gives you a sense of security as you slather on those creams and massage in those moisturizers. But imagine taking that feeling to the next level and feeling confident in those same products because you made them yourself.

All-natural hair products that you can make in your very own kitchen from natural oils, fruits and vegetables provide wonderful benefits to your beauty regimen. The variety of products that you can create is infinite and the best thing about this process is that it's personally crafted.

There are some concoctions that have proven to be extremely effective for black hair, but you can always add or take away from a favorite recipe and customize it to suit your personal hair journey.

You can get in the kitchen and have fun experimenting. You can mix, match, blend, and whip until you find perfection. Your options are limitless.

I began making hair products out of mere curiosity. As I started the process of detoxing internally, I was lead to start minimizing the amount of non-natural products that I used externally. I wanted to nourish my hair with the same things that I used to nourish my organs. I also wanted to be able to use the same products on my young daughters; so I started researching the best options for hair food and got in the kitchen to see what I could come up with.

Here a few of my personal favorite recipes for all-natural hair products that you can create in minutes. They're inexpensive, earth-friendly and can be used on anyone. Some contain as little as one ingredient and others require a bit of extra effort to blend ingredients together, but all are great for natural hair and are gifts from mother earth.

Healthy Hair Essential Oils

Pure therapeutic-grade essential oils are nothing short of miraculous healing potions in tiny bottles. Although there is a scientific principle for the healing properties these oils possess, their capabilities are still very much considered supernatural. With more than 300 choices of oils available to us today, we have no shortage in choosing the perfect oil for our personal needs. Each individual oil has its own healing powers and best uses. From operating as an antiseptic, to healing skin conditions, to stimulating scalp for hair growth, essential oils continually prove to be a "must have" in anyone's beauty regimen.

There are many oils that you can incorporate to promote a balanced environment for your hair. Listen to what your hair likes best. Lavender, peppermint, and rosemary are extremely fond of textured hair and provide great benefits. No matter which essential oils you choose to befriend, be sure to include these three in your rotation.

Lavender is a natural detoxifying essential oil and is extremely effective in promoting healthy environments for hair and skin.

The use of peppermint essential oil dates back to our ancestors in ancient Egypt (Kemet). It possesses many health-promoting properties and is known to stimulate the scalp and encourage hair growth.

Rosemary essential oil is also a great stimulant to the scalp. It increases blood circulation and encourages healthy hair growth.

Essentials oils can be added to any of your hair products or simply mixed into another carrier oil (jojoba oil, almond oil, or olive oil) and massaged onto the scalp as often as needed.

Healing Supplements for Healthy Hair

Horsetail, parsley, and bee pollen are a few holistic supplements that contain healing properties for restoring and maintaining hair health.

For centuries, horsetail has been used as an aid for healthy hair. It strengthens the hair and is very good for split ends. Steeping the dried herb and making a tea is beneficial for hair health. It increases blood circulation and contains numerous other properties for overall health. It is also packed full of calcium, which is effective in preventing hair loss. Although horsetail is full of healing properties, it is very powerful and should not be taken for longer than two weeks at a time.

Parsley contains many nutrients and is extremely beneficial for hair growth and retention. Juicing the leaves and adding some water creates a wonderful tonic that, when applied to scalp, can help cleanse the scalp and treat hair loss. Massaging parsley oil into the scalp is also great for stimulation and promoting hair growth. This treatment imparts softness and shine to your shaft, while controlling dandruff and other scalp conditions.

Bee pollen, known as the "world's only perfect food," contains every nutrient needed by the human body. This vitamin/mineral supplement contains many properties that have been known to increase the health of hair and effectively stimulate hair growth by adding the required amino acids. Heat lowers the nutritional value of bee pollen so avoiding any altered form of this supplement is best. Use the fresh granules by sprinkling them over whole foods or crush them into powder for an acceptable form to use. This method ensures that the vital enzymes remain intact.

The number of herbal supplements, teas, and concoctions available to improve holistic health is immeasurable. Many have been around for centuries and their healing properties have continually proven themselves to be effective. Give thanks for Mother Nature and the gifts She continually gives!

Aloe Vera Hair Gel

The aloe vera plant has numerous amazing natural health benefits. It's packed full of vitamins and minerals and is widely known for its ability to heal wounds and nourish the skin. Because it is about 99 percent water, it has a natural ability to hydrate and moisturize, which makes it great for hair use.

What you'll need:

❖ Aloe Vera plant or 1-3 individual leaves

❖ Vitamin E oil/Essential oils

❖ A sharp knife

❖ An airtight container (preferably glass)

❖ Blender

Directions:

1. Take 1-3 individual aloe vera leaves or remove 1-3 leaves from the bottom of a mature aloe vera plant and place them at a 45-degree angle for a few moments to allow the sticky yellow sap to drain out. Discard any collected Sap.

2. Wash the leaves and carefully cut/peel away the skin to reveal the "gel". For larger leaves, cut into smaller pieces to make peeling easier.

3.   Place gel into blender with a few drops of vitamin E oil and your choice of therapeutic grade essential oils to act as a preservative.

4.   Blend until smooth.

5.   Store in an airtight container and keep refrigerated. (Replace mixture monthly)

6.   Label product with date. Use wooden/plastic spoon to scoop gel out in portions during use to prevent contamination from your fingers.

Flax Seed Hair Gel

Full of nutrients like fiber and omega-3 fatty acids, flax seeds hold a powerful punch for beauty health. Making a hair gel from the seeds lends an all-natural hair product that will leave your hair feeling moisturized and well nourished after styling.

What you'll need:

❖ Flax seeds

❖ Water

❖ Essential oils

❖ Vitamin E oil

❖ Saucepan

❖ Wooden spoon

❖ Airtight container (preferably glass)

❖ Mesh strainer with small holes (small enough to prevent the flaxseeds from slipping through the holes)

❖ Plastic tongs

❖ Measuring cup

Directions:

1. Mix ¼ cup flax seeds with 2 cups of water in medium saucepan.

2. Bring to boil over medium heat for about 10 minutes (stirring occasionally). Water/flax seed mixture will begin to thicken.

3. Carefully remove mixture from heat and immediately strain gel into container to separate seeds. Do not allow mixture to cool as it will congeal.

4. Mix in a few drops of your favorite essential oils and 1 teaspoon of Vitamin E oil to act as a preservative.

5. Store in air container and keep refrigerated for up to 3 weeks.

6. Label product with date. Use wooden/plastic spoon to scoop gel out in portions during use to prevent contamination from your fingers.

Apple Cider Vinegar Rinse

Apple cider vinegar is great for balancing the pH level of your hair and removing product build up.

What you'll need:

❖ Raw unfiltered apple cider vinegar

❖ Distilled water

❖ Plastic cap

❖ Measuring cup

❖ Non-metal mixing bowl/cup/bottle

Directions:

1. Mix 1/3 cup apple cider vinegar and about 1 liter of distilled water. (You can alter this measurement until you find the right ratio for your hair).Cleanse hair thoroughly and saturate with apple cider vinegar rinse. Place hair under plastic cap and let sit for 15 minutes then rinse.

You can leave the apple cider vinegar rinse on hair as a leave-in conditioner for added moisture. Don't worry—the smell will fade away.

Clay Hair Mask

Bentonite clay hair masks are another awesome natural remedy used to remove build up and restore pH balance to hair. It can also be considered a hair detoxifier because it effectively lifts impurities, while conditioning and adding softness to the hair.

What you'll need:

- ❖ Bentonite clay

- ❖ Apple cider vinegar

- ❖ Extra virgin olive oil

- ❖ Essential oils

- ❖ Plastic cap

- ❖ Measuring cup

- ❖ Wooden or plastic bowl

- ❖ Wooden or plastic spoon

Directions:

1. Begin with clean hair. Take ½ cup of clay and slowly add apple cider vinegar to loosen (about ½ cup).

2. Add 1/3 cup extra virgin olive oil.

3.   Add a few drops of essential oils.

4.   Stir ingredients together until smooth.

5.   Add more clay or apple cider vinegar, if needed, to thicken or loosen. Apply to hair.

6.   Cover hair with plastic cap and let sit for about 15 minutes. Do not let it dry completely as it may be difficult to rinse hair clean.

7.   Rinse and condition hair.

Avocado Hair Mask

Widely known as a nutritional powerhouse, avocado holds great benefits for health and beauty. With so many vitamins and minerals, this fruit is the perfect nourishment for hungry hair.

What you'll need:

- ❖ 1 ripened avocado

- ❖ Extra virgin olive oil

- ❖ Wooden/plastic Bowl

- ❖ Wooden/plastic fork or spoon

- ❖ Plastic cap

Directions:

1. Peel and pit avocado, place in bowl and mash.

2. Add 1-2 tablespoons of extra virgin olive oil.

3. Mix/Blend until extremely smooth.

4. Apply to hair and cover with plastic cap and let sit for 15 minutes.

5. Rinse with cool water.

6. Shampoo and Condition as normal.

Nourishing Scalp Massage Oil

Cold-pressed/unrefined (food grade) oils possess many healing properties. The process in which they are created ensures that the nutritional value of each oil remains in tact. They are institutional for hair health, as they are known to stimulate hair growth, prevent hair loss, and retain moisture.

What you'll need:

❖ Jojoba oil

❖ Vitamin E oil

❖ Extra virgin olive oil

❖ Almond oil

❖ Castor oil

❖ Essential oils of your choice is desired

Directions:

1. Mix all oils in equal parts (add a few drops of your preferred essential oils for fragrance or property if desired) and massage into scalp as often as necessary.

* This mixture is also great for use as a hot oil treatment.*

Rosemary and Lavender Spritzer

What you'll need:

❖ Lavender essential oil

❖ Rosemary essential oil

❖ Distilled water

❖ Spray bottle

Directions:

1. Mix 4 oz of distilled water and 5-10 drops of essential oils in spray bottle.

2. Use as often as necessary to moisturize hair and stimulate scalp.

All-Natural Sealants

Raw shea butter and unrefined coconut oil are widely praised for their superb moisture sealing benefits and healing qualities. They are also commonly used for holistic health and beauty treatments.

What you'll need:

❖   Raw Shea Butter

❖   Organic Coconut Oil (unrefined)

Directions:

1.   After cleansing and moisturizing with Rosemary and Lavender Spritzer apply the shea butter or organic coconut oil to seal in moisture.

If you'd like to take this concept a step further, you can melt the shea butter, whip it with a kitchen mixer until fluffy, and add essential oils. You can also add coconut oil directly out of the container to the melted shea butter and mix together for an exotic blend.

Everyone's head of hair was uniquely crafted specifically for them, so don't hesitate in experimenting to see what works best for you. Because there are no chemicals or artificial ingredients within these products, there is no need to fear the creation process. Researching the variety of food grade products that hold substantial benefits for the health of our hair is an amazing adventure, because you'll find that there are so many concoctions to be made.

Have fun with the journey and the process! Listen to your hair and allow it to tell you what it does and does not like. Listen to your spirit and be guided into what ingredients you should mix. The answers are always present when you take a moment to listen. Living a lifestyle of holistic health will positively influence every aspect of your existence. From your daily activities to your hairstyles, balance is the key to vitality.

The Queen

Her throne shimmers with a twinkle of blessings from the Universe.

She is chosen. Chosen to lead a rebellion. A rebellion that will empower the generations of many nations.

Her crown is valued far above what you or I could ever afford within this lifetime or even the next.

She is anointed. Anointed to liberate. A liberating movement to set the minds of her beloved free.

Her garments are woven with fabrics obtained from the celestial souls we see when we're dreaming.

She is called. Called to work. A work so great that her existence is stamped for definition.

Her jewels are a rarity, exclusive and even unattainable to say the least.

She is titled. Titled Queen. A Queen who will leave a legacy of love and untarnished worth.

This Queen. She rules. We must all acknowledge and respect her sovereignty.

It's Time to Shine!

Returning natural is all about the journey. It's about experiencing growth and feeling the moment of expansion. It's about discovering a new *you* and loving every inch of that authentic person.

As we elevate through the concept of Sankofa, we set ourselves, and our future generations, up for greatness. To fully connect with a lineage that proves itself to be phenomenally supreme, no matter what you may have previously known, instills an undeniable pride for self. And with this advancement in knowledge of worth, you ultimately create a mindset that is equipped to accomplish anything you so desire.

Embracing your natural hair while cultivating a natural lifestyle ensures you're not just following a fad and places you on the platform for leadership.

By now, I hope you've realized that you were called to implement change. You were chosen to empower others. You were created to help somebody. There is no better way to accomplish that mission than to know who you are and to walk boldly in that image.

I challenge you to march forward and continue to spread the good news of what returning natural can do for your life. Continue to connect with your ancestors and expand your thinking. Heal those wounds of the past and educate yourself on the truth about black culture. Incorporate a holistic lifestyle regimen into your daily routine and thrive through vitality. Remain in tune with supremacy and get the guidance you need to complete your assignment.

As you grow, share with others. Do *not* fear liberation. For if we do not break the invisible shackles that still bind our mentalities, we will never truly know freedom.

It's your time. Shine bright Super(si)Star. Let your natural hair and your beauty speak. You are an image of God. Radiate!

> **Shoulders back. Chin up. Smiling face.
> Grow deep in love!**

Document Your
Returning Natural Journey

_____'s Journey Journal

These pages will help to document your journey. Use them as a reference to assist with proper maintenance that facilitates holistically healthy hair. Refer back to the entries and use them to encourage yourself as you elevate. Inspire others by sharing your thoughts, concerns, comments and findings.

Date:

General Info:

Mind and Hair (How are you feeling about the journey?):

Body and Hair (Record health and nutrition info):

Spirit and Hair (How are you elevating?):

Products (What is working/not working for your healthy hair routine):

Styles (What styles work for you? What's your "go-to"? Special Occasion? Future styles to try?)"

Concerns/Questions/Comments:

Answers/Resolutions/Knowledge:

Goals:

Plan to achieve goals:

REFERENCES

Afua, Queen. *Sacred Woman: A Guide to Healing the*

    Feminine Body, Mind, and Spirit. New York: One

    World, 2000. Print.

Antol, Marie Nadine. *Healing Teas: How to Prepare*

    and Use Teas to Maximize Your Health. Garden

    City Park, NY: Avery Pub. Group, 1996. Print.

Davis-Sivasothy, Audrey. *The Science of Black Hair:*

    A Comprehensive Guide to Textured Hair Care.

    Stafford, TX: Saja Pub., 2011. Print.

Dictionary.com, n.d. Web. 09 Jan. 2014.

Keith, Velma J., and Monteen Gordon. *The How to*

    Herb Book: Let's Remedy the Situation.

Pleasant

Grove, UT: Mayfield Pub., 1986. Print.

Worwood, Valerie Ann. *The Complete Book of*

Essential Oils and Aromatherapy. San
Rafael, CA:

New World Library, 1991. Print.

ABOUT THE AUTHOR

Nikki Taylor is a public speaker, health and wellness blogger, certified holistic life coach, and owner of The Return Natural Company, LLC. She currently resides in Atlanta, GA, with her husband and two daughters.

Nikki has been passionate about black hair for nearly 20 years and has inspired numerous women to return to their organic beauty. Through her work as a holistic hair care practitioner and natural hair transition coach and stylist, she has made it her mission to promote the acceptance of self through the process of returning natural.

Nikki believes that eating a plant-based diet, vibrating positive light energy, loving genuinely, smiling constantly, laughing often and connecting with nature regularly, is the key to thriving within this realm. She strongly encourages others to do the same.

THE RETURN NATURAL COMPANY, LLC

The Return Natural Company provides products and services that inspire individuals to embrace the vitality of life through holistic living. Digital classes, workshops, books, informational blog posts, and other products that encourage mind/body/spirit balance are available to support and encourage a holistic lifestyle.

Our mission is to deliver information that empowers your mind, nurtures your body, renews your spirit, and promotes self-awareness.

For more information on products and services, please visit www.ReturningNatural.com

ADDITIONAL RESOURCES

List additional resources to help you along your journey. (Example: speakers, educators, hand-made products, hair care consultants, stores/shops to visit, events to attend etc.)